AQUARIUS

AQUARIUS

Let your Sun sign show you the way to a happy and fulfilling life

Marion Williamson & Pam Carruthers

ARCTURUS

This edition published in 2022 by Arcturus Publishing Limited
26/27 Bickels Yard, 151–153 Bermondsey Street, London SE1 3HA

ISBN: 978-1-83940-149-7
AD008771UK

Printed in China

CONTENTS

Introduction

*W*elcome, Aquarius! You have just taken a step towards what might become a lifelong passion. When astrology gets under your skin, there's no going back. Astrology helps you understand yourself and the people around you, and its dazzling insights become more fascinating the deeper you go.

Just as the first humans turned to the life-giving Sun for sustenance and guidance, your astrological journey begins with your Sun sign of Aquarius. First, we delve deeply into the heart of what makes you tick, then we'll continue to unlock your cosmic potential by exploring love, your career and health, where you might prefer to live, and how you get along with family and friends.

Then it's over to gifted astrologer, Pam Carruthers, for her phenomenal birthdate analysis, where she reveals personality insights for every single specific Aquarius birthday.

In the last part of the book we get right inside how astrology works by revealing the different layers that will help you understand your own birth chart and offer the planetary tools to get you started.

Are you ready, Aquarius? You're the zodiac sign most likely to be interested in astrology, so you should enjoy this.

CUSP DATES FOR AQUARIUS
21 January – 19 February

The exact time of the Sun's entry into each zodiac sign varies every year, so it's impossible to list them all. If you were born a day either side of the dates above, you're a 'cusp' baby. This means you may feel like you're a blend of Aquarius/Capricorn or Aquarius/Pisces, or you may instinctively just know that you're one sign right to your core.

Going deeper

If you want to know once and for all whether you're a Capricorn, Aquarius or Pisces, you can look up your birthdate in a planetary ephemeris, of which there are plenty online. (See page 102 for more information). This shows the exact moment the Sun moved into a new zodiac sign for the month you were born.

The Aquarius personality

*Y*ou are a friendly, inventive, erratic person – the zodiac's non-conformist. The astrological symbol for Aquarius is the Water Carrier, usually depicted as a man pouring water from a large vessel. This connection with water has many thinking Aquarius is a Water sign, but it is not – you're a charismatic, idealistic, Air sign, and you spend more time in your head than any other sign of the zodiac.

The symbol for your ruling planet, future-focussed Uranus, is two wavy lines – which again might look like water, but it actually depicts electricity. You're often described as having an exciting, inventive and volatile personality.

Uranus is the planet of sudden change, connected with rebellion, progression and genius technological breakthroughs. Uranus rules over technology, novelty and ingenuity, and, within a birth chart, its position represents originality, personal freedom, excitement and unexpected surprises.

You're a reformer at heart. You look at humanity's customs, traditions and politics and want to change what's not working to create a brighter vision of society – one that's more tolerant and diverse. Your mission is to raise the planet's consciousness by bringing the world's groups and organisations together for the common good.

It can be frustrating for you that, being an Aquarian, you are so ahead of your time that people either ignore, or are not ready to take on, your brilliant ideas. What you think makes sense now will be how the rest of us see it in ten years' time. The same goes for your quirky fashion choices and contrary opinions. You are a person out of step with, and way ahead of, your era.

CURIOUSLY OBSESSIVE

You are intensely curious about how things work, which makes you a gifted researcher, scientist or inventor. You have an erratic style and can mentally juggle many different thoughts at once. But, when you're really interested in someone or something, you're compelled to take it apart, analyse all the different components and put them back together yourself … with a few improvements.

Fascinated by mysteries and esoteric philosophy, subjects such as astrology, ancient religions, conspiracy theories, life in other dimensions or in faraway galaxies, inspire and excite you. You're known for your off-beat tastes and style. If everyone else is getting interested in something, you'll have done it years ago and published a thesis on it. You are tech savvy, quite obsessed with gadgets and the internet. You probably taught yourself how to programme your computer, and you're the first one to know about the latest technological breakthroughs and developments via your friendly network of fellow techie geeks.

Most Aquarians are surgically attached to their phones, and social media would collapse without you – as it combines your favourite things: communication with large groups of people and technology. You can get sucked into internet rabbit holes for days without sleeping or eating properly. Your brain doesn't get tired, if anything your energy and excitement builds the more information you can feed it.

FRIENDLY INFATUATIONS

Your obsessions also apply to people, which can get you into some awkward situations. If someone finds themselves the object of your curiosity, you'll want to know exactly what makes them tick – right down to the nitty gritty – and you can be quite blunt and sometimes a little shocking in your questions. For example, that attractive person you bump into now and then, the musician who lives on a boat … you'll wonder how they make enough money to pay rent. Perhaps they bought the boat outright? How much are boats these days? How do they cope in the winter … and does the drum-playing bring in much cash? Where do they busk? Once you have assembled all the facts, you'll examine your chosen target's personal and psychological explanations and reasoning. If by then the person under your microscope isn't too freaked out, they may suspect you have a bit of a crush. And you do! But it's not the sort they suspect.

You're one of the world's friendliest people, but you can be a little detached from your emotions and this disconnect can cause misunderstandings. Your otherworldly qualities can make you a very glamorous and attractive person, which means that sometimes people you're interested in will get their romantic hopes up. But once you find out everything there is to know about a person, you can become a little disappointed that the mystery wasn't as exciting as you hoped. You might then feel a little embarrassed or explain that you were just being friendly, which could be a bit hurtful for the other party who is no longer the centre of your world. But by then you're gone, lured away by the intense attraction of your new obsession.

TEAM AQUARIUS

One of your contradictions, and challenging life lessons, is that although you see yourself very much as an independent and unique individual, you love being part of a collective. You feel a sense of family belonging in large groups, whether you're all sports fans, members of a social media group, a political protest organisation, or a cosplay fan at a Sci-Fi convention.

You long to lose your sense of identity in a group, yet you can be peculiarly lonely. Romantic relationships can bring up difficult challenges, as you demand the freedom to explore the world in your own way, and don't want to compromise. Ideally, you'll find a partner who will share some of your interests, and who will at least be a member of the groups and clubs you hold so dear. Mutual passions would make your life together a whole lot easier, as sacrificing some of your own time or interests will not be easy for you.

BRILLIANT OR DELUDED?

Sometimes you're so ahead of the game that others stop trying to keep up with your avant-garde thinking or accuse you of plucking ideas from thin air. You can appear distant or distracted and, because you don't connect with people on an emotional level, some may think you've lost the plot or are out of touch. But they're mistaken. You're sharp as nails, perhaps even more so when you're concentrating on something really interesting. Always analysing, your intellectual creativity is drawn from invisible sources that you're probably not even fully conscious of.

You make complete sense to yourself, but if you use that electric mind of yours to read your friends, colleagues, or partner's thoughts, you'll see that sometimes they think you're talking a different language. It may pay off to slow down your thought process just a notch, so that you can communicate more effectively when you need to.

UNEXPECTEDLY STUBBORN

Nobody tells you what to do or think, but if anyone does try to control you, you'll quite calmly do the opposite of what is expected of you. It's just not in your nature to toe the line or stick to anyone else's formula. You are often the catalyst that forces other people to change their ways, and for someone who delights in unsettling the applecart, you're actually rather stubborn.

Once you have decided that you're right about something, there is simply no other explanation available. You're extremely clever, and you may even be in touch with a higher intelligence that not everyone else has access to. But regardless of how you reach your decisions, you believe in your own supreme, sometimes irrational, logic. This is another intriguing Aquarian character contradiction, because you're so keen to see change in society, and are completely open-minded about progress. But when it comes to your own personal behaviour, you'll not budge.

LEO LESSON

Leo is your opposite sign of the zodiac, and you both reflect what the other lacks or needs as well as sharing some similar values. You both need to feel like unique individuals – Leo longs to be a star, living for praise and attention, while you need to feel like a totally independent spirit, but don't give a fig about what other people think of you. But privately, you're in awe of Leo's warmth, generosity and easy affection for everyone they meet. There's no doubt that you are a true humanitarian, and that your intentions to make life better for others are sincere, but you still have to develop your one-to-one relationships. Perhaps subconsciously you are a little afraid that if you give more of yourself to the people you're closest to, that you'll lose a bit of your identity. Leo teaches you that giving of yourself to others completely doesn't diminish you – it makes you shine even brighter.

Aquarius
Motto

GIVE
POWER
TO THE
PEOPLE!

Aquarius in love

*Y*ou're the zodiac's humanitarian, everyone's friend, and you're deeply curious about others. If you're on a date with someone interesting, you often flatter them into thinking you're really interested in them because you ask so many questions. You go into so much detail about their likes, dislikes, and what they had for breakfast that morning, that the other person can be a little bowled over. They could be forgiven for thinking that they might be rather special. And, of course, you think they're rather wonderful, too, but you're probably just as interested in their mother, or the guy with the weird hat on the other table, or the woman playing the piano in the corner of the restaurant. Not everyone is as attentive or curious as you, without hoping things might progress in a romantic kind of way, and your ardent curiosity can inadvertently lead some hopeful people to think they're in with a chance. This can come as something of a surprise to you, though.

DETACHED AND UNSELFISH

You love in a gentle, eternally friendly, way and have an almost scientific interest in the people around you. But you're a bit out of your depth when it comes to physical feelings such as lust, jealousy or passion. As a lofty Air sign, you live in your big eccentric, colourful mind, and go where your eternal curiosity leads you. You're a free spirit, and often when you've discovered everything about the person you're scrutinizing, your attention is grabbed by someone, or something else. Uranus has you firmly focused on the future, so you can hop from an obsession with one person to the next, without much trouble, and can find it baffling when others feel hurt by your fickleness. Unless you have a few Fire or Earth signs in your chart, you don't really get jealous or possessive over people you care about – and don't understand when you've aroused such passions in others. You're unselfish and detached in your affections, thinking everyone is unique in some way, so it's rare for you to feel overtaken by an attraction to one person in particular. But it does happen.

LOVE VERSUS LOGIC

You're delightfully cool and glamorous, and exude an air of mystery, which means you're not short of admirers. But for you to get really hooked on someone they'll probably have an intriguing, rather aloof, air. When you do meet someone who has you entranced, you may be as giddy as a teenager in the first flush of romance, walking along the street bumping into lamp posts. You'll be excited and a little disturbed that you've found someone who is different to everyone else. Though it won't be long before you start analysing what it all really means. You're a supremely logical creature, and love can be a tricky concept for you to get your head around. You think love is just love, caring for humanity as group, looking out for each other as a collective. When one person means everything to you, you'll be perplexed but excited, after all it's a new experience which you will be happy to explore. But you'll wonder what is expected of you in return. Will you have to give up your freedom? Can you commit to one person forever? And so the analysing begins ...

INDEPENDENCE AND COMPROMISE

You're an oddball, Aquarius, you love the weirdest ideas and freely travel the globe pursuing them. You genuinely don't expect other people to move to a Japanese commune, believe in aliens or come to live with you in your converted ambulance. But you're not about to give up any of your strange beliefs or peculiar lifestyle to settle down in a semi-detached house and have a family. That's far too predictable for you, unless you find a workable compromise. Your partner knew what you were like before you committed yourself to one another, so they should already have accepted your need for freedom and independence. If they've stuck with you through your stint as a waterslide tester or an international trampolinist, they'll probably already love this about you, and won't expect you to attend church every Sunday, or sit on the couch every night ... though you may well decide to try either of these for a while, just to prove them wrong!

TRICKY EMOTIONS

You're often embarrassed by emotions – your own and others' – and you'll do your best to keep your own hidden. You tend to dissociate from unpleasant feelings like jealousy, anger, aggression or neediness. But when your logical mind accepts that having to deal with *all* emotions – the dark ones and the beautiful ones – is what makes us human, you'll find there's a nobleness in reasoning that you're only human too.

Most compatible love signs

Libra – gentle, harmonious, romantic Libra can teach you how to love without throwing any awkward emotional tantrums.

Leo – you're in awe of Leo's willingness to please others and secretly think they know something you don't.

Aquarius – you're unique and they're unique. You both don't mind sleeping on futons, plan to build a dwelling out of old car doors, and breed iguanas.

Least compatible love signs

Taurus – Taurus like to know what they're having for dinner tonight, but the last time you ate a regular meal you were in prison!

Scorpio – you're very curious about Scorpio because you know they're hiding something but are afraid to find out exactly what it is.

Cancer – you can't always tell what you did to upset Cancer, but you know it must have been really bad.

Aquarius at work

*I*t may take you a while before you find a career that will keep you interested. You'll happily investigate, experiment and explore while you're young, finding a position that doesn't make you want to staple your fingers to a desk out of boredom. You'll have no trouble being offered work because although your unconventional approach may put some people off initially, they soon discover that you're an eccentric little goldmine.

Your Uranus-ruled mind would be wasted in mundane or routine job, unless you have a large circle of friends there. You thrive in teams and might stick around in a place where you like the people, or if the ethos is right. You're generous with your talents, and you'll happily volunteer your skills in unpaid work for a progressive, or exciting organisation.

You're something of an enigma to your colleagues – cool-headed and distant one minute, and intensely focused and engaged the next. You can be quite pig-headed when you've made up your mind about something too, quite rigidly sticking to your (often outlandish) opinions and expecting others to be on board. Sometimes you can be accused of saying something outrageous just to rock the boat, and being told that 'things have always been done this way' brings you out in a rash.

UNCONVENTIONAL GENIUS

You have something of an absent-minded professor reputation at work. You come up with genius money-making ideas while you're on your tea break but have half an eye on the cricket score in important meetings. It's not that you don't follow rules to be difficult, or shock people deliberately, it's just that your mind is doing something far more interesting and absorbing than remembering when to eat lunch or discovering you're not meant to bring your cat to work. You already know how to run cars on water, teleport to different planets, and cure the common cold – but you got so caught up in your next thought that you forgot to tell anyone about it.

You enjoy being in an office because even though you care not a jot for social conventions, you're a particularly friendly person and your colleagues will think you're a breath of fresh air. When everyone else is wearing smart suits and shiny shoes, you'll be in flip flops with red braces and deerstalker hat. You don't really do anything when it's meant to be done, but somehow what you come up with on the train to work is often as good as what your co-workers produce in a week.

How you actually got the job will be steeped in legend, as you often end up working in different organisations without having formally applied for a position. You may call up a CEO about an idea you've had, to be accused of time-wasting, then offered a job when they discover your little invention could save them a ton of money.

AQUARIUS IN CHARGE

You might be the boss but your unconventional approach to work means you'll probably not look or act like one. You're actually not that comfortable working alone and are more comfortable networking in large groups. You don't want to feel like there's a barrier between you and your colleagues – you want to be amongst them, listening to their ideas, and finding out about their lives. You're not a harsh or strict boss, but you expect them to keep up with you mentally.

You want to make society a better place and you're not afraid to think outside of the box – though some of it is so ahead of time it needs to go back into the box until the rest of the world is ready! You have a radar for what people are about to do and how to improve people's lives with your original solutions. You're not that interested in rank and hierarchy in your job, and you genuinely don't care what other people think of you. It's never all about the money or the status for Aquarius; it's about changing society – ripping up old traditions and customs that are no longer working and replacing them with brilliant new ideas that will revolutionize the planet.

Most compatible colleagues

Libra – you need Libra's diplomacy and understanding of social conventions, as these are something of an alien concept to you.

Gemini – a brilliant mind who likes working on a team – perfect! Just don't expect them to be the same person tomorrow.

Sagittarius – you both have insatiable curiosity and big ideas – together you change the world for the better.

Least compatible colleagues

Aquarius – what planet is this person on? Oh, damn – it's *your* planet!

Aries – these guys can be bossy, while you generally wait for a consensus. They can also be bad tempered, which is not your bag at all.

Capricorn – they're clever, but a bit too conventional to appreciate your genius … and a bit too cynical.

Perfect
Aquarius Careers

Inventor

Astrologer

Alternative therapist

Air traffic controller

Social enterprise professional

Computer programmer

Engineer

Professor

Politician

Scientist

Aquarius
Work Ethic

I SEE YOUR
TRADITIONAL
CONVENTIONS
AND CUSTOMS –
AND I RAISE YOU
A SPACESHIP.

Aquarius friends and family

*C*ompanionship and friendliness are your thing, Aquarius; it's your natural state of being. You're usually a key part of any community, looking out for everyone around you. Shared interests give you a sense of humanitarian purpose, so you'll be a well-known face at local sports clubs, a volunteer at the homeless shelter and a much-loved character in the local pub. You'll likely be the organiser of many different clubs and groups for your local area on social media, and your idiosyncratic ideas and unorthodox fashion sensibilities means everyone knows your face. Sometimes you're the person pushing the dog around in the pram, or you'll be the proud owner of the garden full of ceramic frogs. You'll either have a vintage three-wheeler Reliant Robin parked on your drive, or a state-of-the-art, eco-friendly, electric Tesla.

INDEPENDENT FREE SPIRIT

Transfixed by other people's lives and interests, you delight in good old-fashioned gossip, but you rarely let hearsay cloud your opinion of anyone – if anything, a dodgy reputation just makes people more interesting to you. It's an Aquarius contradiction that, although you are strongly drawn to being part of a team, group or society, you're actually a very private person. You don't usually have intimate friendships with people on a one-to-one basis, perhaps fearing that you may become too responsible for them or want to avoid becoming too entangled in others' lives. Above everything else you require the freedom to act as you please, unimpeded by other people's decisions.

However, you are such a wonderful friend to everyone and think nothing of helping in any practical way possible to make a difference, but you can find it difficult to ask for help when you need it. If you do need assistance, you'll be knocked sideways by the kindness of loved ones – everyone from your brother to the postman would willingly pitch in to lend you a hand. Perhaps if you slowed down a little to let others catch up, you'll see just how appreciated you really are.

AQUARIUS AT HOME

Not bound by traditional gender roles, or indeed any conventions, your home may reflect your love of tech and modern taste. Your ideal pad would be ultra-futuristic, minimalism – all polished steel, glass, large windows and robots to help you vacuum. In reality however, your home environment likely resembles your scattered mind, with discarded machines and computers waiting for you to fix them. You're also one of the most environmentally friendly signs of the zodiac, a purposeful recycler who assigns every piece of rubbish with an inventive new lease of life as building material, furniture, plant pot or hammock.

AQUARIUS PARENT

Before they learn to walk properly, your kids will probably understand how to rewire a plug and change a lightbulb. And they'll certainly know their way around a computer. Your brilliant and eccentric imagination delights your children, whose minds you love to keep alert and curious. You keep your little ones occupied with lively conversation and a plentiful supply of books and puzzles. You'll also be a keen participant in video games and online learning.

AQUARIUS CHILD

Aquarius children enjoy being surrounded by other youngsters as their curiosity about others is how they do most of their learning. They'll feel very much at home when involved with club or group activities such as Scouts, Brownies and sports teams. But they are also highly academic, with scientific minds that soak up technical knowledge like little electric sponges.

Healthy Aquarius

*A*s a mentally-focused Air sign, sometimes you get so caught up in what you're doing that you're genuinely surprised that your body exists at all, never mind that it's complaining it's hungry, or stiff from sitting in the same position. It can be hard for you to get really motivated about moving your body because it can take you away from what you're really interested in.

With inventive, unpredictable Uranus as your ruling planet, your energy levels are usually high, but they can also be erratic. Long nights staring at your computer, or using all your energy trying to solve a scientific puzzle, could leave you feeling frazzled. Sometimes your body appears to just switch itself off for a quick reset … more commonly known to the other zodiac signs as 'sleep'.

Exercise isn't something you like to schedule or think of as routine. You get bored with any repetitive physical movement – and going to the gym at the same time every day won't appeal much. But as an extroverted, social sign of the zodiac, being around others lifts your spirits and fills you with energy, so team sports and busy classes will prove more fulfilling. A bit of a tech nut, you'll be able to source virtual classes or activities too.

FOOD AND DRINK

You don't daydream or wake up thinking of food like some Earth or Water signs, and you have a contrarian approach to nutrition – as you do to everything else too. Why does everyone eat the same old things for breakfast, or eat pudding after dinner? You look at the accepted norms in eating habits and take them apart, which can result in some raised eyebrows from your loved ones. You may have studied nutrition very closely and have a better understanding than most about which vitamins and minerals you really need – and which to avoid. You may have a very progressive attitude to food, eating a pure diet that focuses only on what your body requires, perhaps as a vegan or through practising strict calorie control. Green smoothies after fasting, unpronounceable vegetables from exotic countries for lunch, and a nut-based protein bar designed for astronauts if you feel peckish later. You're an unpredictable eater, and anything too samey annoys you after a while. This might result in some unusual fads, such as existing on caffeine until 3pm, then consuming only red food for two hours, with raw liver before bed.

DISOBEDIENT PATIENT

Naturally rebellious, it's not just food norms you'll question. You'll quibble the knowledge and advice offered by most traditional healthcare givers. Besides, haven't they even heard of emotional freedom technique, past life regression, or reflexology for your headache trouble? You'll do your own research obsessively, and if there's an outlandish theory that fits your current zany idea, you'll try it. Weirdly, the stranger a treatment sounds to you, the more likely it will be to work for you and, as the sign that's so tuned in to the future, you have uncanny premonitions about what therapies might help you or your loved ones.

BODY AREA: ANKLES

Invest in decent shoes, Aquarius, as your ankles, shins and legs (though admittedly rather beautiful) are prone to bumps, twists and breaks. Your bones are thought to be more delicate than the other signs of the zodiac, so try occasionally to turn your constantly whirring mind towards your feet.

Aquarius on the move

*B*eing an independent, free-spirited type, you're a big fan of travel as there's plenty of new people, places and ideas to explore – and it's in your nature to make friends wherever you go. You don't go back to the same place twice and would probably be quickly bored by a relaxing sightseeing tour or beach stay.

Once you've decided where you're going, and with whom, you'll fling a few essentials into a rucksack. Your faith in human nature is touching, and you'll wing it when you're bag packing, thinking other people will share most of the things you'll need. You'll toss your passport, a credit card, the latest mobile phone model and a battery charger, into a rucksack with a freeze-dried NASA protein bar, and hope for the best.

SOCIAL CONSCIENCE

Your strong social conscience and idealistic zeal might draw you to volunteer with an eco-project, or you'll visit somewhere off the beaten track where you'll feel you're contributing to a local economy that needs a helping hand. Trips and holidays with a purpose let you experience new places in a less invasive, more authentic, way and you'll get a warm glow from remembering the people you worked with on your stay. Backpacking appeals to your self-sufficient personality; you're adaptable and hardy, so you don't mind roughing it on a friend's sofa or staying in a hostel for a few nights.

CITIES AND ROAD TRIPS

You're attracted to the energy of big cities too, you've a built-in radar for seeking out vibrant counter-cultures, underground art scenes and interesting social movements. A revolutionary at heart, you sympathise with people pushing to make the world a better place, and you'll gladly volunteer to be part of any progressive movement, if you're in their area.

Going on a road trip with a bunch of pals will also figure high on your list. You prefer travelling in a group to going solo, and you are excellent company on the road. Not only are you a gifted map and sat nav reader, you have a way with machines, so if the car breaks down, you'll find an ingenious way to get it running again – probably fixing the engine with a hairpin.

You're an engaging conversationalist and will keep your friends entertained with your in-depth knowledge of regional history, road networks and geology.

YOUR KIND OF VACATION

For you to get truly excited about a place it has to be exciting, experimental and bring you together with people with similar interests. Going abroad with a group of strangers might be a leap of faith for most, but it's right up your street. You can hook up during the day to camel trek through the desert, plant trees or pick up plastic from a beach, then the night is your own. Rarely alone for long, you'll use your evenings to gen up on the local culture by talking to everyone you meet in cafes and bars. Your inquisitive manner and genuine interest in the lives of other people means you'll be often be invited to their homes, which you take as the highest honour.

Aquarius
Favourite Places

Singapore

Silicon Valley

Kennedy Space Center

Kyrgyzstan mountains

Tree planting venture

Angkor Wat

Eden Project

Area 51, Nevada

Icelandic geothermal power station tour

Sydney

Aquarius
Travel Ethic

I'M SURE IT WILL WORK OUT FINE – SOMEONE WILL DEFINITELY HOST US IN THEIR YURT!

Aquarius
BIRTHDATE
PERSONALITIES

Discover your personal forecast for the day of your birth.

21 January

*Y*ou are a bright and breezy person with a cheerful manner. A brilliant communicator, you are the archetypal traveller on the super-highway that is the internet. Science and computers play an important role in your life and you could be a journalist or work in advertising, as the media invigorates you. A natural mimic, you are witty and great fun to be around so you have a large, ever-changing group of friends. Incredibly restless, your weakness is spreading yourself too thin, always jumping from one new idea to the next and never focussing. In relationships you are easy-going and view your partner as your best friend. They need to be a down-to-earth type who helps keep your feet on the ground. Talking a lot tires you, so chill out with some soothing meditation music.

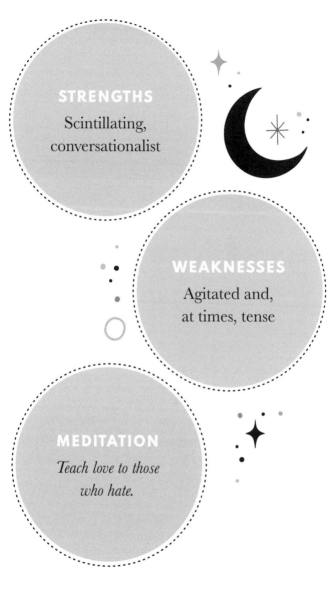

STRENGTHS
Scintillating,
conversationalist

WEAKNESSES
Agitated and,
at times, tense

MEDITATION
*Teach love to those
who hate.*

22 January

Y ou are a sensitive and helpful person with a keen intelligence. You are totally devoted to the truth and to helping people have a better life. Eccentric and unorthodox in your approach, you are essentially well meaning. Being self-employed suits you best, although you are attracted to being part of a small team and social work has enormous appeal. Working for a charity is ideal as long as you are allowed a lot of freedom to implement your original ideas. In personal relationships you can be cool and detached on the outside, but underneath your heart is soft and tender. Emotionally you can suddenly cut off and your partner needs to shower you with affection without being clingy, which takes some skill! Flower remedies are very helpful for you to relax and get in touch with hidden feelings.

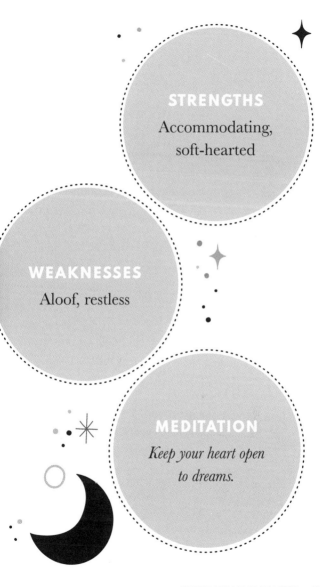

STRENGTHS

Accommodating,
soft-hearted

WEAKNESSES

Aloof, restless

MEDITATION

*Keep your heart open
to dreams.*

23 January

*Y*ou are a flamboyant and creative person who is sincere and honest. You are naturally generous and extremely chivalrous. A born idealist, you are attracted to campaign for social reform. With a regal and dignified manner, you appear to have innate confidence. However, that is not always true as there are times when you lack assertiveness and if you are not in the leadership position you can get very downhearted. Although you can be arrogant at times, your need for affection and admiration makes you vulnerable and very lovable. When you're in love – which is frequently – you shine as romance is second nature to you. However, you can get over-dramatic and sabotage a good relationship because it isn't exciting enough. A thrilling sport such as skiing or snowboarding will lift you out of negative moods.

STRENGTHS
Artistic, valiant

WEAKNESSES
Self-doubting,
self-important

MEDITATION
Begin with the end in mind.

24 January

You are a methodical and industrious person with great capacity for research. With an excellent systematic mind, analysing and synthesizing is what you do best. You have the abilities necessary to be a graphic designer or an astrologer. The mind/body connection fascinates you, and health and healing play an important role in your life, either through personal ill health or the desire to help others. Working in alternative medicine also attracts you. You can be rather clinical at times and people can feel as though you are scrutinising them too closely. In relationships you are friendly and affectionate, but need a passionate partner to set you on fire and bring you out of yourself. You can get lethargic, so a trip to a theme park, with all the thrills of the roller coaster, will infuse you with physical energy.

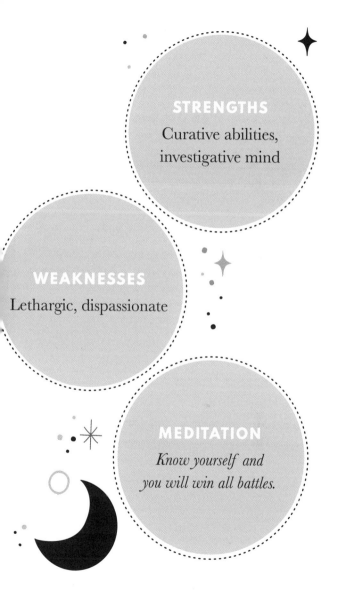

STRENGTHS
Curative abilities,
investigative mind

WEAKNESSES
Lethargic, dispassionate

MEDITATION
*Know yourself and
you will win all battles.*

25 January

*Y*ou are an intellectual and affable person who is artistic and a natural peace-maker. A great observer of people, you are a talented writer and love mixing in literary circles. Dreamy and introspective, you have a magnetism and charm about you. You have a sympathetic nature, are well liked and have a wide circle of friends. At times people aren't sure of your intentions, as you don't like offending anyone, so you will sit on the fence rather than taking sides. Indecision is your bugbear. Your gracious manners make you superb at public relations and you are a naturally good host. In relationships you tend not to communicate your feelings and the best partner for you is a Fire or Water type who helps you explore deep emotions. Pilates is a form of exercise which focusses you on your body and would help ground you.

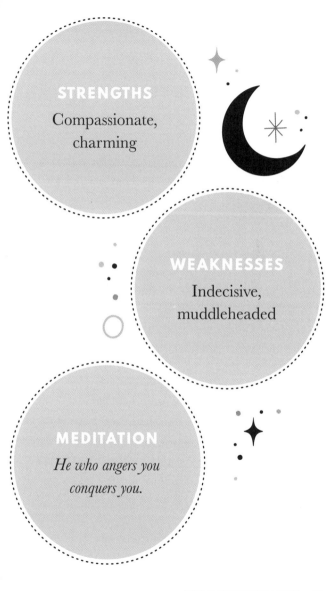

STRENGTHS

Compassionate,
charming

WEAKNESSES

Indecisive,
muddleheaded

MEDITATION

*He who angers you
conquers you.*

26 January

*Y*ou are a powerful and magnetic person with an almost hypnotic quality about you. Extraordinarily charismatic, you are someone who people do not forget easily. You are dedicated to excelling at whatever you do and have amazing stamina. Once committed, you never give up on a project. You pride yourself on doing a thorough job and set high standards. You excel at business, are a brilliant entrepreneur, and are not fazed at handling large amounts of money. Your weakness is jealousy, which comes from a sense of insecurity when young. A committed relationship is the making of you, as you allow yourself to be vulnerable you become more open and loveable. You love the dark and the eclectic, so a rock concert or a jazz club are natural places for you to hang out and enjoy yourself.

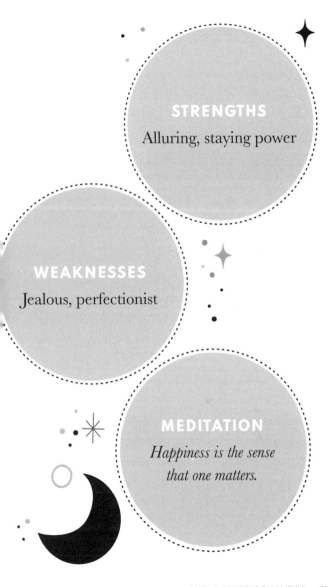

STRENGTHS
Alluring, staying power

WEAKNESSES
Jealous, perfectionist

MEDITATION
Happiness is the sense that one matters.

27 January

*Y*ou are an adventurous and daring person with a pioneering spirit. Highly independent, you do your own thing with considerable originality and self-confidence. Your bold, adventurous spirit is much admired by more timid souls. However, you can charge ahead in your enthusiasm and lack sensitivity to see that you may be treading on others' toes. Your life can evolve in a way that inspires others. A superb teacher, explorer, film or theatre director, your career choices are many and varied. A rolling stone, you have a problem settling down and in your intimate relationships you need a great deal of freedom. Daring sports where you feel challenged are vital if you are at all restricted in your daily life. Hang gliding, skiing or jumping from a plane are just a few you might try.

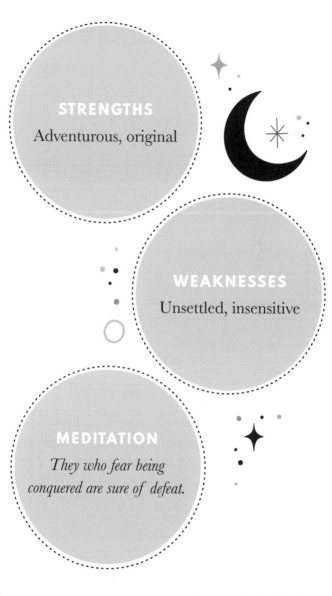

STRENGTHS

Adventurous, original

WEAKNESSES

Unsettled, insensitive

MEDITATION

*They who fear being
conquered are sure of defeat.*

28 January

*Y*ou are an ambitious, hard-working person who has lofty ideals and a desire to make the world a better place. You're a rugged individualist who also has a deep sense of honour and is highly principled. People respect your authority as you communicate well and treat them as your equal. You are broad-minded and although you are generally law-abiding, there is a part of you that rebels and may suddenly act irrationally. Breaking the rules in this way can get you into a lot of trouble. Your creativity is extraordinary and you will spend long hours perfecting your skills. A committed relationship with someone you adore will bring you deep joy. You need to take time out to exercise as you can have problems with stiffness in the joints. Yoga, which increases your flexibility, is ideal.

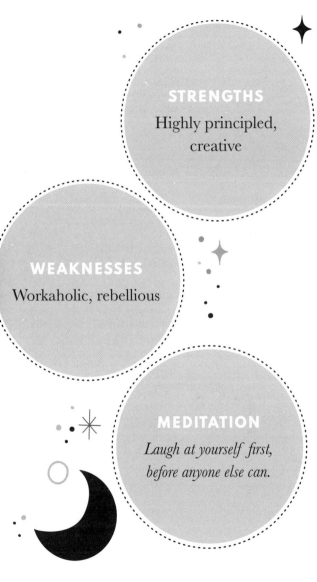

STRENGTHS
Highly principled,
creative

WEAKNESSES
Workaholic, rebellious

MEDITATION
Laugh at yourself first,
before anyone else can.

29 January

You are a clear-headed, logical person with a passion for changing the world. You value the truth above all things and are not afraid of talking about subjects that others find shocking. You are the revolutionary or campaigner whose objective is not to fight, but to persuade others to come round to your point of view. You can be a law unto yourself and incredibly stubborn if people try to force you to do anything against your will. Friends really matter and you love being in groups. You are of a scientific and intellectual bent so you tend to gravitate toward careers where your mind is fully engaged. Intimate relationships are your weakness as it isn't easy for you to connect with deep emotions. A fiery partner can get through your defences and humour always works. A rhythmic exercise like jogging is great for you.

STRENGTHS

Judicious, peaceful revolutionary

WEAKNESSES

Fear of intimacy, bull-headed

MEDITATION

We must never cease from exploration.

30 January

*Y*ou are a gifted communicator and ever-changing person whose intelligence borders on genius. Extremely agile in your thought processes, you pick up new ideas and make connections immediately. You love words and have an extensive vocabulary, so work as a copywriter, playwright or songwriter suits you well. You are an idealist and have a social conscience, so as you mature you feel the need to be useful rather than squander your energy on trivial things. Relationships are your lifeblood as you are essentially a people person. However, intimacy can be uncomfortable as you feel out of your depth when it comes to emotions. Communicating from your heart rather than your head is a lifelong lesson. Yoga is a great way to help you tune into, and become aware of, your body.

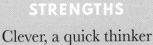

STRENGTHS
Clever, a quick thinker

WEAKNESSES
Scared of deep
emotions, a fantasist

MEDITATION
*Reason and judgement are
the qualities of a leader.*

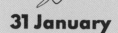

31 January

You are a popular and intelligent person who is both kind and supportive. Very much your own person, you won't follow the rules. You do things differently and can come up with amazingly creative solutions. With a cool exterior, underneath you are warm and caring, and need to feel that what you accomplish has true value. Owning or managing a restaurant or hotel appeals to you as you enjoy nurturing people and giving them an experience they will remember. Your originality needs channelling into something productive or else you switch off and let your moods get the better of you. A childhood sweetheart can be your soulmate as you need a true friend and someone who connects you to your roots. Taking care of yourself by balancing your erratic emotions with acupuncture or homeopathy is a priority.

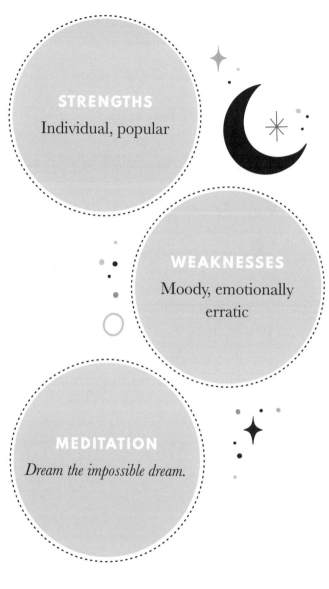

STRENGTHS
Individual, popular

WEAKNESSES
Moody, emotionally
erratic

MEDITATION
Dream the impossible dream.

1 February

*Y*ou are a frank and outspoken person with radical views of how the world can be put to rights. Your intellect is sharp and you are quick to react to hypocrisy, often through the use of humour. You adore poking fun at the establishment and bureaucracy. You can motivate people into action, so politics, with the cut and thrust of debate, is the perfect arena for your talents. A good friend and neighbour, you are the ideal spokesperson for a group. You make friends easily, but because you have so many it is difficult to have a close relationship with anyone in particular. Intimate relationships are not easy as you love freedom and need to be able to do your own thing. You can be highly strung and get burnt out so an exercise like tai chi, which uses your body but stills the mind, is beneficial for you.

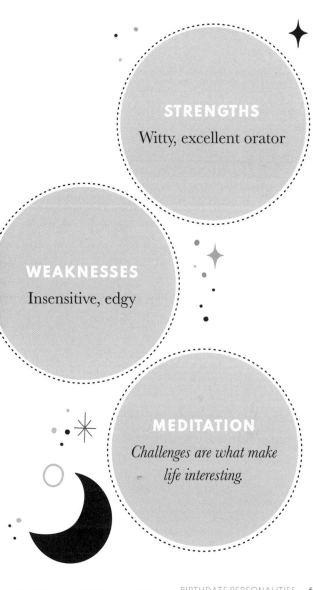

STRENGTHS
Witty, excellent orator

WEAKNESSES
Insensitive, edgy

MEDITATION
Challenges are what make life interesting.

2 February

*Y*ou are a sensual and kind-hearted person with a large dose of originality. You need the comforts of a solid home base and financial security, and work hard to acquire them. You are confident in your abilities and have a high opinion of yourself. This propels you into a position of leadership as you have progressive ideas combined with a practical realism. Some people envy this and find you smug and self-satisfied. However, you enjoy being yourself and tend to ignore what others think of you. Your love life is based on friendship and you need a partner who you respect intellectually. Once you settle down, you are devoted and extremely affectionate and tactile. Bodywork is good for you as you can get sluggish and lethargic; shiatsu or deep tissue massage are ideal.

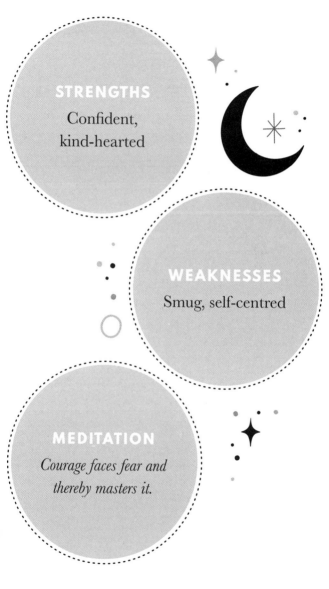

STRENGTHS
Confident,
kind-hearted

WEAKNESSES
Smug, self-centred

MEDITATION
*Courage faces fear and
thereby masters it.*

3 February

*Y*ou are a friendly and light-hearted person with a quick and agile mind. Intensely curious, you love the hustle and bustle of city life. You thrive on the stimulus of meeting new people and exchanging ideas. With a clear, logical mind and honest and reasonable approach, you inspire confidence in others. You are a great negotiator, as you are able to see things from a higher perspective. Public relations, journalism and advertising are all suitable careers. However, you are an ideas person and need others to handle the practical details. Easily bored, you are always moving on to the next challenge. Your relationships can be very cerebral, so learning about emotional intelligence would be highly beneficial for you. Turning off the computer in the evening is crucial if you want your mind to relax.

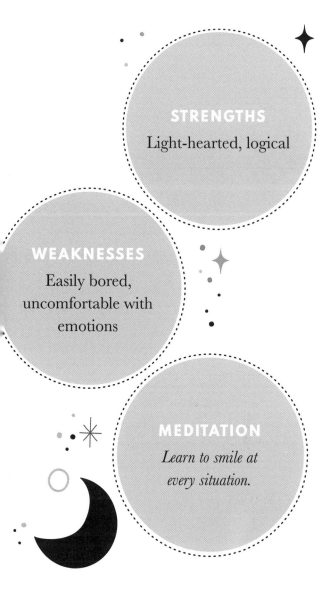

STRENGTHS
Light-hearted, logical

WEAKNESSES
Easily bored,
uncomfortable with
emotions

MEDITATION
*Learn to smile at
every situation.*

4 February

You are an altruistic and thoughtful person with a strong urge to change things for the better. You're the campaigner who firmly, and with clear expression, voices what others can't or won't say. Working for an aid organization or a charity is ideal for you. Deeply connected to your early home life, your own personal story is the basis for your idealism and shows your ability to share yourself with others. Your weakness is a tendency to sulk or use tears to get your own way. A relationship which provides warmth and a sense of security – yet also allows you room to express your individuality – is the solution. You love kitchen gadgets and experimenting with exotic styles of cooking, which is a delightful way for you to find contentment and peace within.

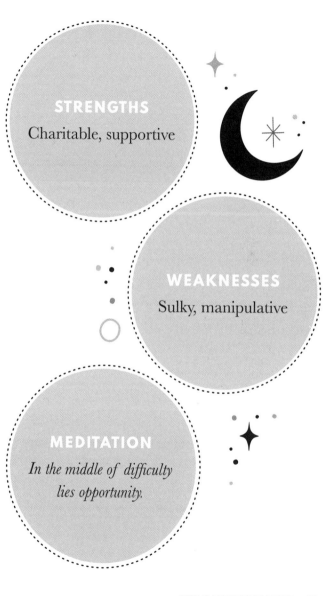

STRENGTHS
Charitable, supportive

WEAKNESSES
Sulky, manipulative

MEDITATION
In the middle of difficulty lies opportunity.

5 February

*Y*ou are an inspired person with the potential to be a creative genius. You are a visionary who takes on new ideas enthusiastically and can be an accomplished inventor. With a strong sense of individuality, you need to express your uniqueness through creative work. Never the shrinking violet, you naturally take the lead. An important aspect of your drive to succeed is to see your name 'up in lights'. Acting, whether professionally, or as an amateur, is very fulfilling for you as you need to feel feted by others. However, you can be vain and take great offence if people ignore you. Love plays a large part in your life and you always believe the best of your partners. This can lead to you being deeply disappointed, so you rely heavily on your friends to console you. Channel your heartbreak into creativity; it will reward you.

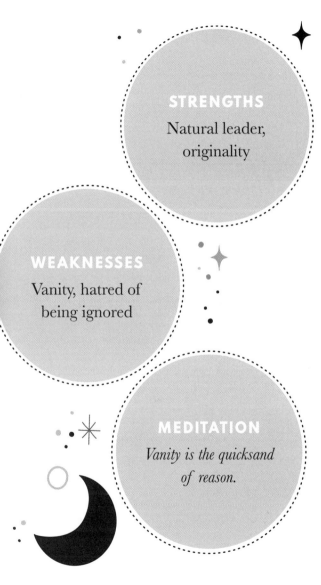

STRENGTHS
Natural leader,
originality

WEAKNESSES
Vanity, hatred of
being ignored

MEDITATION
*Vanity is the quicksand
of reason.*

6 February

You are a kind and thoughtful person with a love of organising. You aim to be useful and are a humanitarian at heart, so healthcare is a good industry for you. Always finding new methods and systems to make life easier, you are excellent at office or hospital administration. You love the efficiency of computers and will be up to date with the latest technology. Perfectionism is your weakness as your standards are so high. A bit of a paradox, you can be very gregarious and also at times a loner. In relationships you are an affectionate and gentle lover, and you need someone who tenderly encourages you to explore your sensual nature. Getting messy is so contrary to your nature that it is actually a great way for you to release your inhibitions. Mud wrestling may be a stretch too far, but you get the idea!

STRENGTHS

Thoughtful lover,
efficient

WEAKNESSES

Introverted, an idealist

MEDITATION

*Live – because life is
everything.*

7 February

You are a stylish and eccentric person who enjoys a rich social life. People-watching and chatting with friends are your favourite pastimes. A lover of beauty, you are superbly suited to working in the arts or the fashion industry. With a gift for mimicry and a cosmopolitan sense of humour, you can shock others, but in the best possible way, with no intention of hurting them. You are an innovator and part of the avant-garde set. If people take advantage of your good nature and kindness, you can be quite forthright in stepping away from your involvement. A born lover, relationships are the breath of life for you. However, you can over-intellectualize your partner and neglect to connect with them emotionally. You often stay up late socializing with friends, so need some quiet time at home relaxing, listening to music or reading.

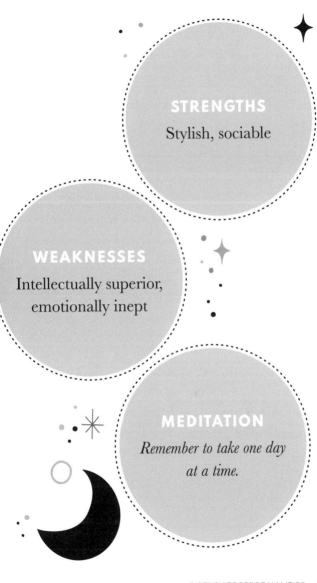

STRENGTHS

Stylish, sociable

WEAKNESSES

Intellectually superior,
emotionally inept

MEDITATION

*Remember to take one day
at a time.*

8 February

You are an intense and brooding person with a sense of mystery about you. Your enigmatic personality is compelling and draws people to you. As a tremendous actor, or working in business, your strong will and confidence in your abilities commands respect and admiration. People can even be overwhelmed, and view you with a sense of awe. On the downside, you are capable of using your powers to gain advantage over others and may be ruthless in your desire for success. You also have a tendency to seek more freedom than is realistic. In a committed relationship your sensuality and passion can be expressed as long as you choose a partner who understands your complexity. Exploring caves or going on a murder mystery weekend are the kinds of activities that turn you on.

STRENGTHS
Passionate, mysterious

WEAKNESSES
Manipulative, ruthless

MEDITATION
With hope, you can get through the toughest times.

9 February

You are an avant-garde and worldly person with a huge zest for life. Incredibly enthusiastic and open to experiment, you are a risk-taker and a bit of a daredevil. Well suited to being an entrepreneur, you are unlikely to be able to stick to a regular office job. Your vast imagination and future-orientated way of thinking lends itself to work on innovative projects. What you lack is patience and attention to detail, so you need someone else to check for mistakes. You mix in a wide circle of bohemian types and have many friends from different cultures. Your intimate relationship has to be based on intellectual rapport and your partner needs to have the same adventurous spirit as you. Trekking or camping in the wilderness is your idea of a fun weekend.

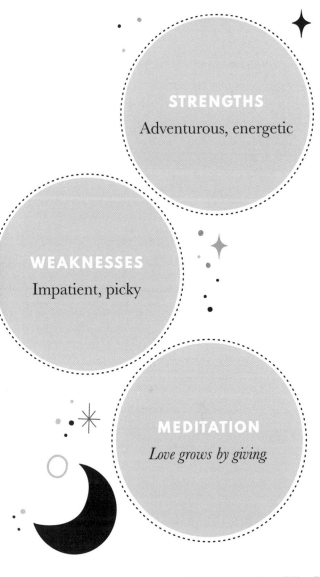

STRENGTHS
Adventurous, energetic

WEAKNESSES
Impatient, picky

MEDITATION
Love grows by giving.

10 February

You are a self-sufficient, independent person with a great deal of common sense. You have a realistic approach to life and are immensely disciplined. With crystal-clear thinking, you set goals and will work your utmost to attain them. Supremely ambitious, you have a stoical acceptance of what it takes to get to the top and your personal life can suffer as a result. You are attracted to working in policy or for a think-tank as you are always looking to the future. You are friendly and charitable and will offer practical assistance to those in need. In relationships you need an equal and someone who can shake up your somewhat Spartan attitude. Humour is your soft spot and a stand-up comedy night or trip to the theatre to see a funny play can help to revitalize and balance you.

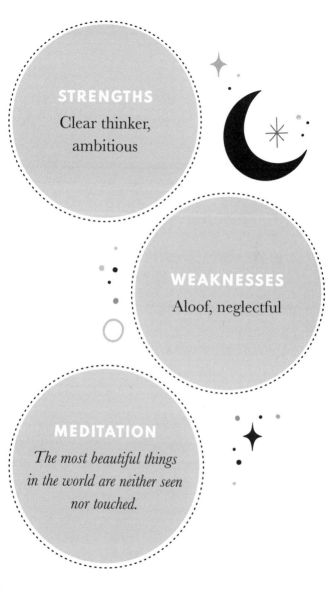

STRENGTHS
Clear thinker,
ambitious

WEAKNESSES
Aloof, neglectful

MEDITATION
*The most beautiful things
in the world are neither seen
nor touched.*

11 February

You are a quirky and offbeat person who is eminently sociable. You have the ability to be a friend to all types of people from all walks of life. People warm to your eccentric ways and the sense of camaraderie that you create. You are an innovator – whether in the world of engineering, computing or fashion – and your creativity makes its mark. Always controversial, your life is never dull. You are restless and crave novelty; you are prone to get up and leave abruptly if bored. In relationships you can try to fit your partner into a mould and need to learn to listen rather than fix them. With a tendency to be highly strung, you seek a distinctive form of exercise that releases nervous tension. Experiment with martial arts such as qi gong, kendo and karate until you find the ideal one for you.

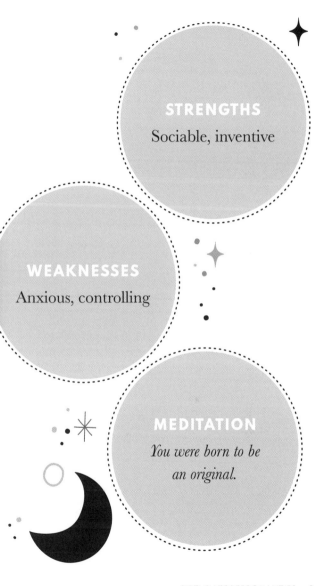

STRENGTHS
Sociable, inventive

WEAKNESSES
Anxious, controlling

MEDITATION
*You were born to be
an original.*

12 February

*Y*ou are an imaginative and realistic person who can get along with all sorts of people. Your natural sympathy and compassion touches people's hearts and they feel you are their friend. Your understanding nature, combined with your intelligence, takes you into the caring and medical professions. There is a strongly spiritual side to you and you may experiment with psychic studies, tarot or astrology. You would also make a brilliant interfaith minister. A weakness is your tendency to daydream and suddenly drift off into another realm, and you definitely hold a utopian vision of how the world could be. An intimate relationship needs to combine friendship with unconditional love, which is a tall order for anyone to fulfil. Music is the ideal way to lose yourself in reverie, undisturbed by mundane reality.

STRENGTHS
Benevolence, sagacity

WEAKNESSES
Dreamer,
high expectations

MEDITATION
The journey is the reward.

13 February

*Y*ou are a controversial and fascinating person with an engaging and provocative manner. You love to rebel against the status quo and shock people, yet paradoxically you have a soft, romantic side. If you fulfil your potential you can become incredibly successful and really make a difference to the world. Expressing the caring and kind-hearted side of your nature is vital and social work suits you, as does writing poetry. If you get pulled down by your negative emotions you can be maudlin and fall victim to addictions. A gift of whacky humour can lift you and others up. In relationships you can be vulnerable and when you mature you realize just how rewarding being supported emotionally is for you. A sport like golf, that acts like a walking meditation, is a godsend.

STRENGTHS
Enchanting, good
sense of humour

WEAKNESSES
Overemotional,
negative

MEDITATION
*Act as if what you do
makes a difference.*

14 February

*Y*ou are a passionate and idealistic person who lives life to the full. You have a grand, romantic vision of life and are able to express yourself with creative flair and originality. Always experimenting, you can live on the edge, and are not averse to taking risks. You can blow hot and cold and need to find a way to express your strong emotions. This energy is best channelled into a cause that you believe in and you make an excellent defender of the underdog. You gravitate towards groups as you love to take centre stage, so you are the ideal political leader. In an intimate relationship you need to be adored and in return you are tremendously loyal. Your energy can dip suddenly and you need to protect your nervous system with herbal remedies rather than chemical stimulants.

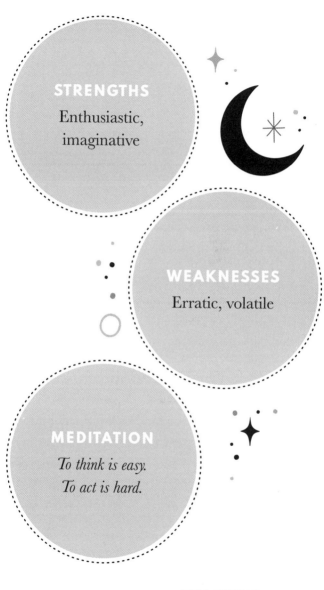

STRENGTHS
Enthusiastic, imaginative

WEAKNESSES
Erratic, volatile

MEDITATION
To think is easy.
To act is hard.

15 February

You are a kind and devoted person who has a love of routine. Your ability to dissect problems, clearly organize your thoughts, and then come up with constructive solutions, make you a great architect or designer. You also possess technical skills and you can take up dressmaking and carpentry. If a friend wants to declutter, then you are the right one to help. You are a purist and like nothing better than cleaning and throwing stuff away. However, you can take over and become overly critical about the way people live. To have a successful relationship you need to learn that you cannot control everything. You make a loving and nurturing parent, who knows how to fuel the imagination of children. Learning massage is a wonderful way for you to give and receive the physical affection you need.

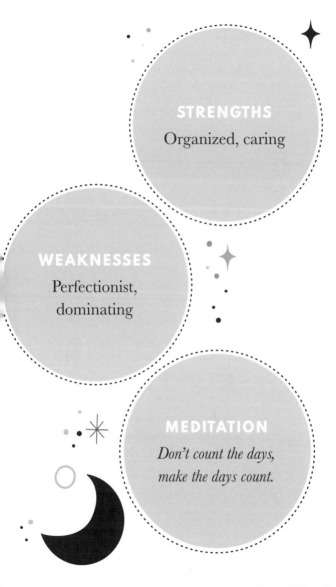

STRENGTHS
Organized, caring

WEAKNESSES
Perfectionist,
dominating

MEDITATION
*Don't count the days,
make the days count.*

16 February

You are a charming and well-mannered person who is a true humanitarian. You have a high IQ and are very knowledgeable. Cultured and civilized, you are naturally drawn to the art world and museums where your intellect is stimulated. You are immensely talkative and need the stimulus of city life and a variety of sophisticated people around you, although the countryside gives you inner peace. Your true purpose is fulfilled when you find a cause you can support that improves the quality of people's lives. In love you can be over-idealistic and subject your partner to unrealistic expectations. For a long-term relationship, you need someone who can be firm with you, while allowing you to express yourself. Singing in a choir would be a wonderful way for you to connect you with your emotions.

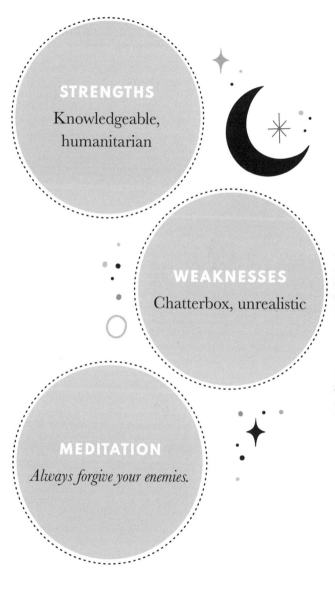

STRENGTHS

Knowledgeable, humanitarian

WEAKNESSES

Chatterbox, unrealistic

MEDITATION

Always forgive your enemies.

17 February

*Y*ou are a deep and fascinating person who lives life to the full. You love to probe and discover the hidden aspects of people, starting with knowing all about yourself. Being psychoanalysed at an early age is likely, and it could become your career. Your mind is razor-sharp and you love investigating with scientific precision, yet there is also a dark and sensual side to your nature. You are self-reliant and a born survivor with immense resilience. However, you can detach yourself from people and shut down as an emotional defence mechanism. In relationships it's all or nothing and you need a partner who matches your intensity, or you can get obsessed with your own self-importance. Gardening or renovating your home can be the best physical exercise because you achieve something satisfying while doing it.

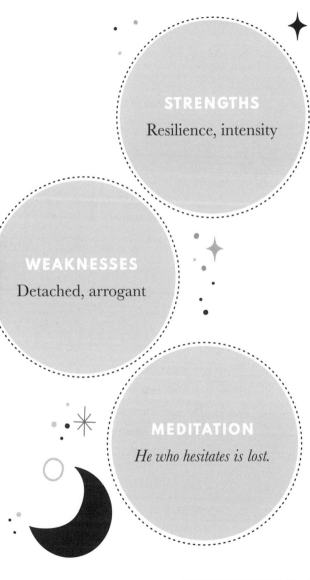

STRENGTHS

Resilience, intensity

WEAKNESSES

Detached, arrogant

MEDITATION

He who hesitates is lost.

18 February

You are an electrifying, optimistic person with a daring vision. You have an outrageous sense of humour and a passion for travel and new experiences. A larger-than-life character, people take notice of you. You can't bear to be hemmed in and are constantly breaking new ground in your desire to know everything. Philosophy and anthropology are just two subjects that might be the foundation of your career. You make a superb teacher as you have a fine grasp of complex concepts. Always promoting your pet cause, you can be over-moralistic, often ending up preaching to anyone who'll listen. Domestic life is not for you, so your personal relationships tend to be free and open as you value your independence so highly. The best present anyone could ever give you is flying lessons.

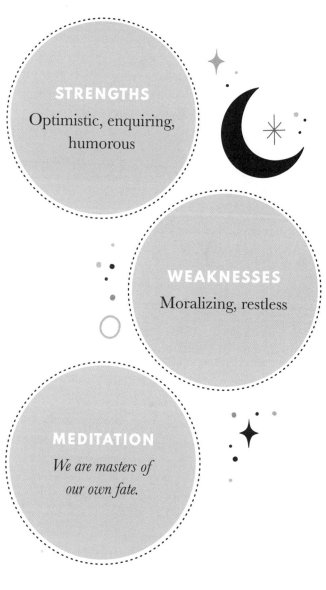

STRENGTHS

Optimistic, enquiring, humorous

WEAKNESSES

Moralizing, restless

MEDITATION

We are masters of our own fate.

19 February

*Y*ou are an honest and dependable person with shrewd business acumen. A deep thinker with a future-orientated outlook, you are guaranteed to come up with inspired solutions to the most difficult problems. You are well suited to a management position or teaching, where you can use your talents as a wise mentor. A team player, you see the best in people and can help them find their true vocation. You're a true egalitarian and a natural at working with all sorts of people. In relationships, you can remain cool and detached and you certainly don't go in for dramatic displays of emotion. Your partner needs to be able to lure you away from the workplace. You love being surprised, so letting your lover treat you to a fine meal at a restaurant with an unusual cuisine has great appeal.

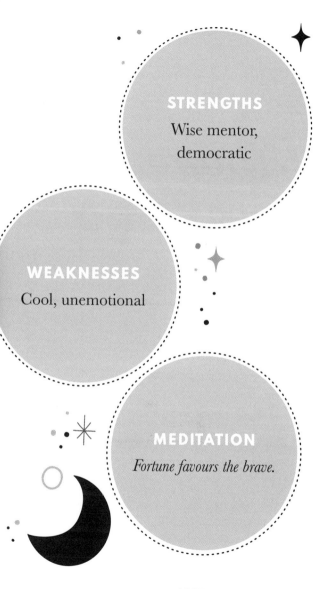

STRENGTHS
Wise mentor, democratic

WEAKNESSES
Cool, unemotional

MEDITATION
Fortune favours the brave.

Going
DEEPER

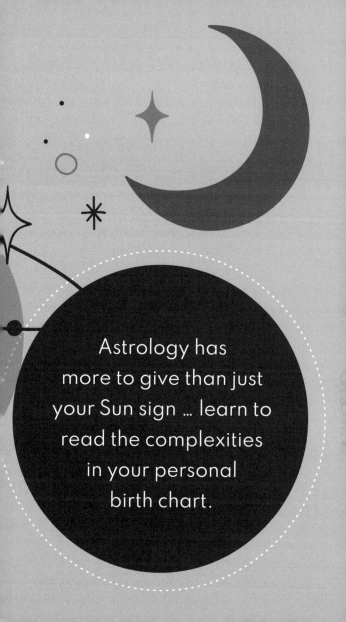

Astrology has more to give than just your Sun sign ... learn to read the complexities in your personal birth chart.

Your personal birth chart

*U*nderstanding your Sun sign is an essential part of astrology, but it's the tip of the iceberg. To take your astrological wisdom to the next level, you'll need a copy of your unique birth chart – a map of the heavens for the precise moment you were born. You can find your birth chart at the Free Horoscopes link at: www.astro.com.

ASTROLOGICAL SYNTHESIS

When you first explore your chart you'll find that as well as a Sun sign, you also have a Moon sign, plus a Mercury, Venus, Mars, Jupiter, Saturn, Neptune, Uranus and Pluto sign – and that they all mean something different. Then there's astrological houses to consider, ruling planets and Rising signs, aspects and element types – all of which you will learn more about in the birth chart section on pages 112–115.

The art to astrology is in synthesising all this intriguing information to paint a picture of someone's character, layer by layer. Now that you understand your Aquarius Sun personality better, it's time to go deeper, and to look at the next layer – your Moon sign. To find out about your own Moon sign go to pages 104–111.

THE MOON'S INFLUENCE

After the Sun, your Moon sign is the second biggest astrological influence in your birth chart. It describes your emotional nature – your feelings, instincts and moods and how you respond to different sorts of people and situations. By blending your outer, Aquarius Sun character with your inner, emotional, Moon sign, you'll get a much more balanced picture. If you don't feel that you're 100% Aquarius, your Moon sign will probably explain why!

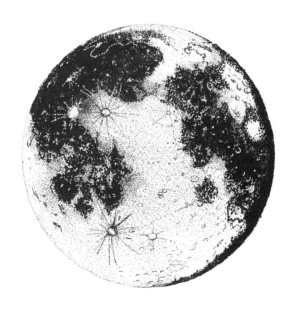

Aquarius with Moon signs

AQUARIUS SUN/**ARIES MOON**

You're a humanitarian, friendly person, free-thinking and inventive. You're a quick problem solver and can get impatient if others don't keep up with your brilliant ideas. You're a fast mover too, good at sport with a great deal of physical energy to burn and you're probably restless and a bit of a fidget. Your passionate Aries Moon gives you a quick temper and a rebellious streak, and your Aquarian Sun can't stand to see injustices in the world. Working in a career where you help others to be more self-sufficient would be ideal. You are a romantic soul at heart who thrives in a dynamic, stimulating partnership, as long as there is plenty of space for you to be yourself.

AQUARIUS SUN/**TAURUS MOON**

An intriguing mix of sensible, down-to-earth Taurus and original, inventive Aquarius. To the outside world you are an original, even quirky person, keen to try new things and happy to pursue a different path to everyone else. But emotionally you crave stability, a steady relationship, and dislike change. Taurus and Aquarius are both stubborn zodiac signs with fixed ideas about what's right and wrong in the world, but your Aquarian curiosity means you'll enjoy exploring different ways of living, as long as you have some home comforts, or a solid plan of action. Your Venus-ruled Moon warms your friendly but aloof Uranus-ruled Sun, making you more likely to maintain long-term relationships. Taurus Moon people are usually good with money, which balances out your Aquarian absent-mindedness when it comes to paying bills on time.

AQUARIUS SUN/**GEMINI MOON**

 You're an extremely inventive and curious person who loves experimenting with interesting theories – and sometimes downright eccentric ones. You're tuned into the zeitgeist and are brilliantly intuitive about what tomorrow will bring, so much so that you rarely feel rooted in the present moment. A charismatic and thoughtful individual, you probably have many friends and admirers, although you may feel a little bewildered in emotional situations. Gregarious and helpful, you like being in the spotlight and are less comfortable on your own. You march to the beat of a different drum, and value your freedom of expression highly – which can make it a real challenge for you to fit into other people's routines and lifestyles. You may decide to live in a different house, or country, to your partner and choose to have a rather unconventional relationship.

AQUARIUS SUN/**CANCER MOON**

 With an emotionally sensitive, caring Cancer Moon, your cool, logical Sun is softened, giving you an intuitive, empathic quality. You have a broad intellect and are fascinated by what makes people tick, and your knack of getting under people's skin to see the real person is valued by all your loved ones. Like all Aquarians you'll have plenty of idiosyncrasies, but you'll likely still wish to have a family and a secure home base. You will be fiercely protective of the people you love and some of the usual Cancer shyness will be countered by your Aquarian curiosity in people. You're a determined and tenacious person with bags of business sense, and your slightly offbeat personality attracts a wide circle of friends and associates.

AQUARIUS SUN/**LEO MOON**

 You were born on a full Moon when the Sun and Moon were in opposite signs of the zodiac. Polarising signs share similarities but also have fundamental differences.

Proud and talented, you have a strong sense of who you are and what you want to achieve. You have a big heart and a broad mind, and probably have lofty aspirations. You're cool and logical in a crisis, and, a bit of a rule breaker, you often take an unconventional approach to problem solving. Your Aquarian Sun doesn't care what other people think and tends to push you through any barriers or obstacles without checking on what's expected of you. But your Leo Moon is a populist, wanting to gain everyone's approval before making decisions.

AQUARIUS SUN/**VIRGO MOON**

 You're an idealistic and helpful person, brilliantly well organised and a little eccentric. An unconventional mix of absent-minded Aquarius and detail-focussed Virgo means you are capable of flipping from total concentration to complete absent-mindedness. Your mind is rarely still, and you can grasp both logical and esoteric concepts with ease. You're skilled in seeing the whole picture, including all the little details, which can prove both inspiring and overwhelming. With your Uranus/Mercury combination you probably love a puzzle, or solving other people's problems, and your Virgo Moon naturally draws you to helping others improve. You may appear emotionally distant to people who don't know you well, but loved ones see your softer underbelly and appreciate that you're always harder on yourself than anyone else.

AQUARIUS SUN/**LIBRA MOON**

 You're a progressive and charming double Air sign personality. You have big ideas and the communication skills to put them into practice. Friendly, with a large social circle, you love being in a group of people and can understand many different people's opinions at once. Your Libra Moon ensures you take time to make fair decisions, even if that takes you a long time. You're open to unusual and even downright eccentric points of view, and your Aquarian Sun means you'll tolerate society's rebels and underdogs. You might not be the most practical person when it comes to making plans or following a routine, but you're thoughtful, friendly and humanitarian. Your Libra Moon will make you something of a hopeless romantic, and you'll be happiest in a committed partnership.

AQUARIUS SUN/**SCORPIO MOON**

You're a powerful character – intellectual and emotionally intense. Scorpio Moons like to keep their feelings to themselves, so you'll probably show nothing on the surface, even if you're burning with feeling inside. This can be tricky for your chillier, detached Aquarian Sun, which prefers to keep things logical, and finds heated feelings to be alien territory. You'll be able to pick up on others' emotions easily and will have something of a sixth sense when you feel someone is trying to hide something from you. Resourceful and clever, you have reserves of energy that keep you going even though the most difficult of times, and you always learn from your experiences. Your Aquarian side makes you sociable and enjoy being in groups, and you are deeply curious about what interests other people.

AQUARIUS SUN/**SAGITTARIUS MOON**

You're an open-minded and intellectually curious person, keen to push boundaries and explore new possibilities. You dislike feeling restricted and you have big dreams. Practicalities are often overlooked in your search for truth and meaning, but you're such an optimistic, fearless character that the finer details won't bother you for too long. You're a born explorer and you wish to understand other people's deepest held beliefs, which takes you to the four corners of the globe. Your philanthropic, idealistic Moon compliments your eccentric, intellectual Sun, and given the financial and intellectual freedom, you'll find ingenious ways to make life better for people in difficult circumstances. You're warm, generous and tolerant and will be happiest with a partner who is as freedom-loving as you.

AQUARIUS SUN/**CAPRICORN MOON**

You're a level-headed and practical person with a quirky sense of humour. You're a realist but you're not conventional. You may decide to follow an unusual path through life, but your determination to succeed makes you one of life's true pioneers. People may underestimate your friendly eccentricity at first, but loved ones will know you succeed at anything that takes your fancy. You can often make life a little difficult for yourself by choosing the path less travelled, but you are able to show others that you can be exactly who you want to be without having to follow the tried and tested route. You are very connected to your roots and family, and have an affinity with older people, having a deep appreciation of their wisdom and experience.

AQUARIUS SUN/**AQUARIUS MOON**

As a double Aquarian, you're one of a kind. Never dull, you have a surprising answer to everything. Unpredictable and sometimes irrational, it can be hard to fathom you out. If you feel pushed in any particular direction, you'll randomly change course just to see what happens. You're not a planner or terribly practical but your brilliant mind often draws you to scientific or engineering careers, preferably jobs that require an inventive approach. You have an enjoyable social life and important friendships, but when it comes to personal relationships you can be erratic. You like the freedom to change your mind as often as you make decisions, and you'll work with a best lover who shares your unconventional attitude and love of change.

AQUARIUS SUN/**PISCES MOON**

You are probably attracted to unusual ideas and beliefs, which will take you on an unconventional path through life. Your compassionate and intuitive Pisces Moon gives you a spiritual outlook on life, and you'll be curious about philosophy, religion and psychic matters. You sense there is more to life than your Air Sun sign logic likes you to believe, and you'll probably dabble in alternative therapies and beliefs throughout your life. You like to feel unencumbered by a conventional lifestyle but you also feel very attached to the people you love. One of life's true romantics, you believe that the power of love can solve all of life's problems and will crave a deep and lasting bond with a partner who feels the same way.

Birth charts

*L*earning about your Sun and Moon sign opens the gateway into exploring your own birth chart. This snapshot of the skies at the moment of someone's birth is as complex and interesting as the person it represents. Astrologers the world over have been studying their own birth charts, and those of people they know, their whole lives and still find something new in them every day. There are many schools of astrology and an inexhaustible list of tools and techniques, but here are the essentials to get you started ...

ZODIAC SIGNS AND PLANETS

These are the keywords for the 12 zodiac signs and the planets associated with them, known as ruling planets.

 ARIES
courageous, bold, aggressive, leading, impulsive

Ruling planet
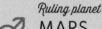 MARS
shows where you take action and how you channel your energy

TAURUS
reliable, artistic, practical, stubborn, patient

Ruling planet
VENUS
describes what you value and who and what you love

GEMINI
clever, friendly, superficial, versatile

Ruling planet
MERCURY
represents how your mind works and how you communicate

CANCER
emotional, nurturing, defensive, sensitive

Ruling planet
MOON
describes your emotional needs and how you wish to be nurtured

LEO
confidence, radiant, proud, vain, generous

Ruling planet
SUN
your core personality and character

VIRGO
analytical, organised, meticulous, thrifty

Ruling planet
MERCURY
co-ruler of Gemini and Virgo

LIBRA
fair, indecisive, cooperative, diplomatic

Ruling planet
VENUS
co-ruler of Taurus and Libra

SCORPIO
regenerating, magnetic, obsessive, penetrating

Ruling planet
PLUTO
deep transformation, endings and beginnings

SAGITTARIUS
optimistic, visionary, expansive, blunt, generous

Ruling planet
JUPITER
travel, education and faith in a higher power

CAPRICORN
ambitious, responsible, cautious, conventional

 Ruling planet
SATURN
your ambitions, work ethic and restrictions

 ## AQUARIUS
unconventional, independent, erratic,
unpredictable

 Ruling planet
URANUS
where you rebel or innovate

 ## PISCES
dreamy, chaotic, compassionate, imaginative,
idealistic

 Ruling planet
NEPTUNE
your unconscious, and where you let things go

The 12 houses

Birth charts are divided into 12 sections, known as houses, each relating to different areas of life as follows:

1 FIRST HOUSE

associated with *Aries*

Identity – how you appear to others and your initial response to challenges.

2 SECOND HOUSE

associated with *Taurus*

How you make and spend money, your talents, skills and how you value yourself.

3 THIRD HOUSE

associated with *Gemini*

Siblings, neighbours, communication and short distance travel.

4 FOURTH HOUSE

associated with *Cancer*

Home, family, your mother, roots and the past.

5 FIFTH HOUSE

associated with *Leo*

Love affairs, romance, creativity, gambling and children.

SIXTH HOUSE

associated with *Virgo*

Health, routines, organisation and pets.

SEVENTH HOUSE

associated with *Libra*

Relationships, partnerships, others and enemies.

EIGHTH HOUSE

associated with *Scorpio*

Sex, death, transformation, wills and money you share with another.

NINTH HOUSE

associated with *Sagittarius*

Travel, education, religious beliefs, faith and generosity.

TENTH HOUSE

associated with *Capricorn*

Career, father, ambitions, worldly success.

ELEVENTH HOUSE

associated with *Aquarius*

Friends, groups, ideals and social or political movements.

TWELFTH HOUSE

associated with *Pisces*

Spirituality, the unconscious mind, dreams and karma.

THE ELEMENTS

Each zodiac sign belongs to one of the four elements – Earth, Air, Fire and Water – and these share similar characteristics, as listed below.

EARTH

Taurus, Virgo, Capricorn

Earth signs are practical, trustworthy, thorough and logical.

AIR

Gemini, Libra, Aquarius

Air signs are clever, flighty, intellectual and charming.

FIRE

Aries, Leo, Sagittarius

Fire signs are active, creative, warm, spontaneous, innovators.

WATER

Cancer, Scorpio, Pisces

Water signs are sensitive, empathic, dramatic and caring.

PLANETARY ASPECTS

The aspects are geometric patterns formed by the planets and represent different types of energy. They are usually shown in two ways – in a separate grid or aspect grid, and as the criss-crossing lines on the chart itself. There are oodles of different aspect patterns but to keep things simple we'll just be working with four: conjunctions, squares, oppositions and trines.

CONJUNCTION

0 degrees apart
intensifying

SQUARE

90 degrees apart
challenging

OPPOSITION

180 degrees apart
polarising

TRINE

120 degrees apart
harmonising

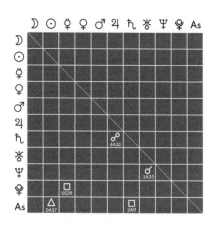

Planetary aspects for Matt's chart

HOUSES AND RISING SIGN

Each chart is a 360° circle, divided into 12 segments known as the houses (see pages 116–117 for house interpretations). The most important point in a birth chart is known as the Rising sign, which shows the zodiac sign on the Eastern horizon for the moment you were born. This is usually marked as ASC or AS on the chart drawing. This is the position from where the other houses and zodiac signs are drawn in a counter-clockwise direction. The Rising sign is always on the dividing line of the first house – the house associated with the self, how you appear to others, and the lens through which you view the world.

CHART RULER: The planetary ruler of a person's Rising zodiac sign is always a key player in unlocking a birth chart and obtaining a deeper understanding of it.

A SIMPLE BIRTH CHART INTERPRETATION FOR AN AQUARIUS SUN PERSON

BIRTH CHART FOR MATT, BORN 18 FEBRUARY 1991 IN WEXFORD, IRELAND.

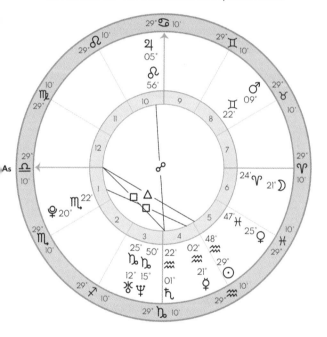

THE POSITION OF THE PLANETS: Matt has Libra rising. The Sun is in Aquarius, the Moon is in Aries, Mercury is in Aquarius, Venus sits in Pisces, Mars is positioned in Gemini, Jupiter's in Leo, Saturn occupies Aquarius, Uranus and Neptune are in Capricorn and Pluto occupies Scorpio. Also note the house positions that the planets are in.

INTERPRETATION BASICS

How do you begin to put all these signs and symbols together? It's usually best to begin with the Sun, Rising sign (As), and then to examine the condition of the Moon sign.

SUN, MOON, RISING SIGN (AS) AND CHART RULER: Matt's Sun (creativity/core personality) was positioned in rebellious, inventive Aquarius when he was born, and it was in the fifth house (creativity/joy). This is a lively, energetic combination, which indicates a changeable, unusual person (Aquarius) who is deeply creative and values his freedom (fifth house). Matt's Aries (passion/energy)Moon (feelings) in the sixth house of work and routines, shows that he probably puts a great deal of emotional energy into his work, and that he needs to feel organised to feel secure. His Rising sign (As) is in relationship-oriented Libra, so he's likely to approach the world (Rising/As) in a diplomatic, graceful way. His chart ruler is Venus (Libra's ruler) and is in the fifth house (spontaneity/self-expression) in Pisces (empathy/impressionability). This means he needs to express himself in a loving (Venus) creative, emotional (Pisces) manner, and probably has artistic talent or a love of music, dance or theatre. Matt will likely be attracted to the softer/gentler (Pisces) aspects of others' personalities and share a love of film, painting or photography.

OTHER PLANETS: Matt's Mercury (communication) is in Aquarius and occupies his fourth house of home and family. Perhaps Matt's parents have a strong influence on the way he thinks – or he is mentally connected with his roots or the past (fourth). He probably isn't attracted to a traditional home life (Uranus). His Mars (drive/action) is in wordy Gemini in the eighth house (mystery/resources. This placement indicates Matt could have a forthright manner and a real passion (Mars) for communication (Gemini). He finds a way to get through to people on a very deep level (eighth).

Jupiter (luck/fortune/enjoyment) is in Leo in the tenth, which is a powerful influence and a strong indicator of worldly success. He's happy being in the spotlight (Leo) – this would be an auspicious position for an actor or entertainer. Matt's Saturn occupies Aquarius in the fourth house, which can indicate an authoritative (Saturn) parent (fourth), or perhaps Matt found his home life to be restrictive or challenging.

With both Neptune and Uranus in his third house of communication, Matt may have an idealistic (Neptune) and original (Uranus) way with words. And as both planets are in business-minded Capricorn, he should be able to use these skills to attract money or success.

ADDING IN THE PLANETARY ASPECTS

Let's take a brief look at the strongest aspects – the ones with the most exact angles or 'orbs' to the planetary degrees (the numbers next to the planets).

SUN TRINE RISING SIGN (AS): Matt's core personality (Sun) is in tune (trine) with others (Rising/As) and he ought to attract good fortune through his nuanced relationship skills.

PLUTO SQUARE MERCURY: Matt may feel less powerful (Pluto) when he's in challenging situations (square) and has to speak or express his opinions (Mercury).

SATURN OPPOSES JUPITER: When Matt wants to explore and expand his world (Jupiter) he may encounter restrictions or challenges (opposition) at his work, or from authority figures (Saturn).

SATURN SQUARE RISING SIGN (AS): Matt encounters challenges (square) when his aproach to life (Rising/As) is overly cautious or he is slow to act (Saturn).

NEPTUNE CONJUNCT URANUS: This is a strong (conjunction) visionary (Neptune) and progressive (Uranus) aspect that Matt can use to his advantage throughout his life.

YOUR JOB AS AN ASTROLOGER

The interpretation above is simplified to help you understand some of the nuts and bolts of interpretation. There are almost as many techniques and tools for analysing birth charts as there are people!

Remember when you're putting the whole thing together that astrology doesn't show negatives or positives. The planets represent potential and opportunities, rather than definitions set in stone. It's your job as an astrologer to use the planets' wisdom to blend and synthesise those energies to create the picture of a whole person.

Going deeper

To see your own birth chart visit: www.astro.com and click the Free Horoscopes link and then enter your birth information. If you don't know what time you were born, put in 12.00pm. Your Rising sign and the houses might not be right, but the planets will be in the correct zodiac signs and the aspects will be accurate.

Further reading and credits

WWW.ASTRO.COM

This amazing astrological resource is extremely popular with both experienced and beginner astrologers. It's free to sign up and obtain your birth chart and personalised daily horoscopes.

BOOKS

PARKER'S ASTROLOGY by Derek and Julia Parker (Dorling Kindersley)

THE LITTLE BOOK OF ASTROLOGY by Marion Williamson (Summersdale)

THE BIRTHDAY ORACLE by Pam Carruthers (Arcturus)

THE 12 HOUSES by Howard Sasportas (London School of Astrology)

THE ARKANA DICTIONARY OF ASTROLOGY by Fred Gettings (Penguin)

THE ROUND ART by AJ Mann (Paper Tiger)

THE LUMINARIES by Liz Greene (Weiser)

SUN SIGNS by Linda Goodman (Pan Macmillan)

Marion Williamson is a best-selling astrology author and editor. *The Little Book of Astrology* and *The Little Book of the Zodiac* (Summersdale 2018) consistently feature in Amazon's top 20 astrology books. These were written to encourage beginners to move past Sun signs and delve into what can be a lifetime's study. Marion has been writing about different areas of self-discovery for over 30 years. A former editor of *Prediction* magazine for ten years, Marion had astrology columns in *TVTimes*, *TVEasy*, *Practical Parenting*, *Essentials* and *Anglers Mail* for over ten years. Twitter: @_I_am_astrology

Pam Carruthers is a qualified professional Vedic and Western astrologer and student of *A Course in Miracles*. An experienced Life Coach and Trainer, Pam helps clients discover the hidden patterns that are holding them back in their lives. A consultation with her is a life enhancing and healing experience. She facilitates a unique transformational workshop 'Healing your Birth Story' based on your birthchart. Based in the UK, Pam has an international clientele.

All images courtesy of Shutterstock and Freepik/Flaticon.com.